"The Lion's Heart Series"™

LET GO ⊛F the BULLY

Using EFT and Matrix Reimprinting

TANYA DE VILLIERS

ILLUSTRATED BY MARILIE FOUCHÈ

FOREWORD

In this exciting second book from the Lion's heart series, Tanya de Villiers manages to give young children the ability to see bullying from a different perspective. With great rhyming and superb illustrations the readers' attention is captured instantly. Simple explanations are used to explain important concepts and convey positive new messages. EFT and Matrix Reimprinting are used as a foundation coupled with movement to facilitate letting go. This book is a fantastic visual tool for parents, therapist and teachers.

Karl Dawson, Creator of Matrix Reimprinting, Hay House Author

It was a sunny day for some

and a gloomy day for others.

While walking on the playground the Lion saw a dreadful sight.
Gorilla was pushing Giraffe and Hippo in a bid for a fight.

Giraffe started

to cry and

Hippo gave a

very long sigh.

The school bell rang and all the kids ran...

except for Giraffe and Hippo. Their eyes

were still red from crying because of

Gorilla's behaviour. Let's call him Fred.

4

The Lion came closer and the two looked up.

They said,
        "Please help! This bullying must stop!"

5

With a swirl and a twirl the Lion took out his magic wand.
"Are you ready to let it go and bury the bully in the sand?"

"Bury? The bully? In the sand?
You must be mad. No we cannot!
It would be wrong, and besides, he
is very strong."

"No", said the Lion. "That is not what I mean!

We will not bury Fred the bully, but rather the bully inside of you."

"I am not a bully!"
said Giraffe and
started to cry.

"Neither am I."
said Hippo, again
with a sigh.

9

"I know you are not bullies. Let me make it clear. Where do you feel fear in your body when the bully is near?"

"Point with your finger" said the Lion.

"I feel it in my stomach and sometimes in my throat" said Giraffe staring at his broken toy boat.

"Sometimes I feel it in my heart" said Hippo, "because it starts to pound away. I sometimes grab my chest in case my heart doesn't want to stay."

"Exactly" the Lion roared.
"That is why I said, the bully is not
just on the outside, although he is real,
but he is also on the inside
because that is where you feel."

"What about his words? They hurt me so.
Fred says I have the biggest nose, the
longest neck, the ugliest toes and that
I look like a shipwreck!"

Hippo looks down, as if she is ashamed.

"Fred says I am so big that for earthquakes I must be blamed."

15

"I can show you how to feel better. Will you try it with me? Who knows what good things might happen?"

"Come on, let's see."

"How big is this feeling that the bully brings?"

"Take your magic hand (We all have one you know?), tap on the side of the hand and say..."

"Even though I don't know why this is happening to me, I am being bullied and that is not what I want for me. I would like it to stop and let go of it quickly."

Now take your hand, tap on top of your head and say: "I feel so unsafe. The world is not a safe place for me."

I feel so unsafe... The world is not safe for me...

Why is he picking on me?

Tap between your eyebrows and say: "Why is he picking on me?"

Tap on the side of the eye: "Is it because what he said is true, or does it come out of the blue?"

Tap lightly with two fingers under the eye: "He makes me doubt myself and I lose faith in myself."

Tap with your fingers under the nose: "He makes me feel unloved."

Under the chin: "He makes me think that I am not good enough and a coward for not sticking up for myself."

21

Tap on the chest :
"I feel so mad,
frustrated,
confused and sad."

Tap on top of your head:
"Is it him or is it me?
Who is the
one that
needs to
believe?"

22

"Now turn to the left and
then turn to the right."

"Put your head on your shoulder and point

your arm. Now draw

an eight laying on its

side. Follow your

finger with your

eyes and repeat

five times."

23

"Take a deep breath and blow all the bad feelings out."

"Show me again how big the feelings are and point with your finger."

"If you aren't feeling better, do it a few more times. You can use your own words and it doesn't have to rhyme."

Tap on the side of the hand

Tap on top of your head

Tap between your eyebrow

Tap on the side of the eye

Under the eye

Under the nose

Under the chin

Tap on the chest

Tap on top of your head

Now turn to the left and then turn to the right

Put your head on your shoulder and point your arm. Now draw an eight laying on its side

"I feel a little better but how will that change Fred? They say he is so mean that he uses his cat for a bed."

"A Bully is someone who doesn't feel good and would like everyone to feel like he does. He feels alone but he wants to feel strong" said the Lion.

"He likes the attention even when it is wrong."

"A bully's power is hidden in how he makes you feel. Feelings are a choice we make and that makes the bully real."

"Would you like to help Fred and tell him how you feel?" asked the Lion.

Giraffe jumped back and said:
"You must be mad!
He will twist my neck into a wheel."

30

"Now close your eyes and take a deep breath. Think of Fred, come on do your best."

31

"Can you see him in your mind?

Tell him how you feel."

"You make me feel horrible, ugly and weak. You hurt me very deep. To think we were friends on the first day of school, then something happened and you became mean. I became your enemy , or so it would seem."

33

"Is there something that Fred
would like to say?" asked the Lion.

"Can we tap on Fred while thinking in your minds? Now look at the picture and tap on his face."

Tap on his head: "Fred, I don't know why you do this and why you have to hurt me so?"

Eyebrow : "All I know is that the bullying must stop let this silliness go."

Side of the eyes: "You can be great, you know?"

Under the eyes: "You can even make new and wonderful friends."

Under the nose: "But this silliness must end, it must stop."

Under the chin: "You don't have to make others feel bad so that you can feel better."

Tap on the chest: "Great friends will always make you feel better."

Top of the head: "I forgive you and its time to let go. No more will your words and actions affect me so."

"If you can imagine giving him a hug and setting the bully free,
what colours can we add to make it more beautiful to see?"

Giraffe points at red. Hippo wants
a rainbow.

"Is there something
else that we can add, to make the picture
right for you and take away the sad?"

"How about friendly faces to know
that you aren't all alone?" said the Lion.

"How about an armour
made of steel so that no words can
hurt us, and all the good can
stay on the inside." said Giraffe.

"The strongest armour is made of love.
You must love yourself from head to
toe to truly let all the bad feelings go."
said the Lion

"I can love myself." said Hippo.

"O yes and so can I." said Giraffe.

"Now let's wrap that picture in love and let it fly through our heads to our hearts, in our bodies to every single part."

"Can you feel yourself tingle?
Can you feel yourself smile?"

"Take another deep breath and again, blow out all that is left and not supposed to be there."

The second bell rings ...

...and now our friends must go.

"Remember" said the Lion, "some things take time but now you have a special power. One that you can quickly do in the shower."

"One that can let you decide, what you want to let in, let near, and what you would like to change and let go."

www.ingramcontent.com/pod-product-compliance
Lightning Source LLC
Chambersburg PA
CBHW041517280526
45792CB00004B/1281